MY COMMUNITY

A TRIP TO THE RECYCLING CENTER

Sara Milner

PowerKiDS press

New York

Published in 2017 by The Rosen Publishing Group, Inc.
29 East 21st Street, New York, NY 10010

First Edition

Editor: Melissa Raé Shofner
Book Design: Mickey Harmon

Photo Credits: Cover Ariel Skelley/Getty Images; p. 5 Education Images/UIG/Getty Images; p. 6 Stockbyte/Getty Images; p. 9 (main) Bloomberg/Contributor/Bloomberg/Getty Images; p. 9 (recycling symbol) Bohbeh/Shutterstock.com; p. 10 Monty Rakusen/Getty Images; p. 13 safacakir/Shutterstock.com; p. 14 Dave and Les Jacobs/Getty Images; p. 17 DAJ/Getty Images; p. 18 puifaiminiiz/Shutterstock.com; p. 21 Akimov Igor/Shutterstock.com; p. 22 kirin photo/iStockphoto.com.

Library of Congress Cataloging-in-Publication Data

Names: Milner, Sara, author.
Title: A trip to the recycling center / Sara Milner.
Description: New York : PowerKids Press, [2017] | Series: My community | Includes index.
Identifiers: LCCN 2016027784| ISBN 9781499427783 (pbk. book) | ISBN 9781508152958 (6 pack) | ISBN 9781499430080 (library bound book)
Subjects: LCSH: Recycling centers–Juvenile literature. | Recycling (Waste, etc.)–Juvenile literature.
Classification: LCC TD792 .M555 2017 | DDC 363.72/82–dc23
LC record available at https://lccn.loc.gov/2016027784

Manufactured in the United States of America

CPSIA Compliance Information: Batch #BW17PK: For Further Information contact Rosen Publishing, New York, New York at 1-800-237-9932

CONTENTS

This is the recycling center.

RECYCLE
Recycling Center
Recycling Machines
Hours of Operation
8:00am – 5:00pm
Hours of Operation
100% RECYCLED

WE
RECYCLE

Paper goes in the box.

A **truck** brings the paper.

DO YOUR BIT

Workers sort the paper.

New paper is made.

People bring **cans**.

The cans are cleaned.

Machines crush the cans.

New cans are made.

Recycling helps Earth.

WORDS TO KNOW

cans

paper

truck

INDEX

WEBSITES

Due to the changing nature of Internet links, PowerKids Press has developed an online list of websites related to the subject of this book. This site is updated regularly. Please use this link to access the list: www.powerkidslinks.com/mycom/recycle